PAMPHLETS ON AMERICAN WRITERS · NUMBER 40

UNIVERSITY OF MINNESOTA

Arthur Miller

BY ROBERT HOGAN

UNIVERSITY OF MINNESOTA PRESS · MINNEAPOLIS

Printed in the United States of America at
the North Central Publishing Company, St. Paul

Library of Congress Catalog Card Number: 64-64447

second printing, revised 1967

PUBLISHED IN GREAT BRITAIN, INDIA, AND PAKISTAN BY THE OXFORD UNIVERSITY
PRESS, LONDON, BOMBAY, AND KARACHI, AND IN CANADA BY THE COPP
CLARK PUBLISHING CO. LIMITED, TORONTO

ARTHUR MILLER

Robert Hogan, who teaches English at the University of California, Davis, is the author of *The Experiments of Sean O'Casey* and *After the Irish Renaissance: A Critical History of the Irish Drama since* THE PLOUGH AND THE STARS. He has also edited *Seven Irish Plays, 1946–1964.*

✗ *Arthur Miller*

Sᴏᴍᴇ ᴘʟᴀʏᴡʀɪɢʜᴛs have complained that the drama is one of the more naive forms of art, and many, many playwrights have complained that dramatic criticism is one of the most naive forms of criticism. Probably a prime example of that critical naiveté is the centuries old and apparently fruitless battle about the nature of tragedy. In our time that battle has hovered around the cliché that tragedy cannot be written in the modern world. Modern man, so the argument goes, has shriveled in stature; his society has somehow lessened the significance of his soul in contrast to Athenian or Elizabethan society which apparently did not make moral dwarfs of Athenians or Elizabethans. In this view, modern man is equated with Elmer Rice's Mr. Zero or one of Rossum's Universal Robots. Naturally, the events which happen to such ciphers can scarcely have the intensity of meaning of those events which happened to Oedipus and Lear.

Most of the interesting modern playwrights have fortunately paid very little attention to this view and have quietly gone about their business of creating a large and significant repertory of plays. Despite sporadic attempts, impelled mainly by the critics, to return to traditional forms, most of the interesting modern playwrights have plowed new fields. Endeavoring to create a drama equal in intensity to tragedy, they have either turned away from tradition entirely or utilized it in some fresh fashion. Mythology in modern dress, symbolism, expressionism, that neo-expressionism called vaguely the Theater of the Absurd, and that absurd theater called vaguely the poetic drama have all had their champions. Certain pre-eminently brilliant dramatists, such as Strindberg and Shaw, could create the tragic effect by other types of plot and in a much less traditional manner than that discovered by Aristotle in the dramas of Sophocles. However, the triumphs of Strindberg and Shaw did not invalidate Aristotle's perception; they merely emphasized that there are two tragic traditions in the Western world — the austere and the experimental.

Perhaps the austere tradition may be most easily traced by the plot structure that Aristotle discovered in *Oedipus Rex*. Certainly, considering structure alone, one may easily see that Euripides, Shakespeare, O'Casey, and Tennessee Williams belong to one tradition, and Sophocles, Racine, Ibsen, and Arthur Miller to another. Yet the plays of Miller have more than a merely structural similarity to those of Sophocles and Racine and Ibsen. Like the plays of those earlier men, Miller's also vitally embody the austere tragic spirit. That embodiment, in a time which is overwhelmingly eclectic and experimental, gives the real meaning and the real importance to the work of Arthur Miller.

Arthur Miller was born on October 17, 1915, in the Harlem section of Manhattan. His father was a prosperous manufacturer, and his mother, herself the daughter of a manufacturer, had been a teacher in the public school that Miller attended in Harlem. Miller was such a poor student that, although his teachers looked him up in their records after he had become a notable playwright, none of them could actually remember him. He failed many subjects, including algebra three times. He was more interested in sports than in school, and later remarked, "Until the age of seventeen I can safely say that I never read a book weightier than *Tom Swift*, and *Rover Boys*, and only verged on literature with some of Dickens."

The family fortunes having been lost in the crash of 1929, Miller went to work after high school in an automobile parts warehouse on Tenth Avenue in Manhattan. During this time he picked up a copy of *The Brothers Karamazov* under the impression that it was a detective story and read it on the subway to and from work. The book made such an impact upon him that he determined to be a writer, and for two and a half years he saved thirteen dollars a week from his fifteen-dollar salary in order to finance a year in college. Finally, after some eloquent letter writing on his part, he was admitted to the University of Michigan as a journalism student. He managed to maintain himself in college by a small salary as night editor of the *Michigan Daily*, by aid from the National Youth Administration, and by an occasional prize won by his writing. In college he began to write plays and twice won Michigan's Avery Hopwood Award. One of these prize plays, *The Grass Still Grows*, also won the Theatre Guild National Award of $1250 in 1938.

Miller received his B.A. in 1938, and returned to New York to work with the Federal Theatre Project in its last months. For the project he wrote a comedy, but plans for its production were abandoned when Congress did not appropriate funds to continue the theater. Out of a job, Miller turned to writing for radio as well as to working in the Brooklyn Navy Yard and in a box factory. In 1940 he married Mary Grace Slattery whom he had met in college, and they subsequently had two children.

Miller did not relish writing for radio. The medium had too many taboos and restrictions, and its scripts had to be short and almost banally simple. As he remarked to a *New York Times* interviewer in 1947, "I despise radio. Every emotion in a radio script has to have a tag. It's like playing a scene in a dark closet."

Although radio in the 1940's was a wasteland as vast as the television of today, Miller found in it more freedom than did many other writers. He did not have to grind out unvarying and unending segments of *Portia Faces Life* or *Fibber McGee and*

Molly, for much of his work was done for *The Cavalcade of America* and *The Columbia Workshop*, two series which offered some opportunity for variety and originality. Actually, his many scripts must have served as a kind of artistic discipline, for he became skillful enough to pound out a completed half-hour script in eight hours.

A few of Miller's radio scripts have been published. Their intrinsic merit is not enormous, but they show a freshness fairly rare for radio, and they help to refute the notion of Miller as a totally humorless conscience of his race. "The Pussycat and the Expert Plumber Who Was a Man" is a light, Saroyanesque fantasy about a talking cat who blackmails some influential politicians into letting him run for governor. Two of the speeches suggest the central preoccupations of Miller's mature work. At one point Tom the cat remarks, ". . . the one thing a man fears most next to death is the loss of his good name. Man is evil in his own eyes, my friends, worthless, and the only way he can find respect for himself is by getting other people to say he's a nice fellow." This concern is precisely what bedevils John Proctor at the end of *The Crucible* and Eddie Carbone at the end of *A View from the Bridge.* This premise — that the most valid and fertile subject for the drama is the attempt to show man struggling to be at one with society — is basic to all of Miller's work up to *The Misfits.*

Miller has frequently discussed this theory. For instance, in his essay "On Social Plays," prefacing the 1955 edition of *A View from the Bridge*, he wrote that this social concern was the primary one of the Greek tragic writers and that the attempts of modern dramatists to show man striving for his individuality could end only in meaningless case histories. He wrote: "The social drama, as I see it, is the main stream and the antisocial drama a bypass. I can no longer take with ultimate seriousness a drama of individual psychology written for its own sake, however full it may be of insight and precise observation. Time is moving; there is a world to make, a civilization to create that will move toward the only goal the humanistic, democratic mind can ever accept with honor. It is a world in which the human being can live as a naturally political, naturally private, naturally engaged person, a world in which once again a true tragic victory may be scored." Without such a social basis, the drama, he thought, would turn to its "true opposite, the antisocial and ultimately antidramatic drama." This was written in the mid-1950's before some of those plays of Tennessee Williams which seem most truly the dramatic extension of one man's individual psychology, and before the great flux of antisocial dramas which have been lumped together under the description Theater of the Absurd.

This preoccupation is interesting to find in Miller as far back as 1941, but his solution to the problem then was considerably simpler than what he could later accept. In "The Pussycat and the Expert Plumber Who Was a Man," Tom is exposed by an expert plumber named Sam and explains his exposure by remarking, "a cat will do anything, the worst things, to fill his stomach, but a man . . . a man will actually prefer to stay poor because of an ideal. That's why I could never be president; because some men are not like cats. Because some men, some useful men, like expert plumbers, are so proud of their usefulness that they don't need the respect of their neighbours and so they aren't afraid to speak the truth." In his mature plays up to *The Misfits*, Miller postulated that men do need the respect of their neighbors. It is this need that makes John Proctor retract his lie and Eddie Carbone insist upon his.

Another of Miller's radio scripts, "Grandpa and the Statue," has less merit than "The Pussycat," but the theme that man needs society is more evident. Grandpa Monaghan refuses to contribute money for the pedestal for the Statue of Liberty, and the story shows how he learns that his decision was wrong. He finds that he needs the society and must be an integral part of it, and the statue comes to symbolize for him all that he inarticulately feels.

A third radio play, "William Ireland's Confession," is a droll historical script about the author of some notable Shakespearean forgeries. Its psychology is simplified for radio, but it is not a bad script. This radio play, and a patriotic one about the war-time merchant marine, "The Story of Gus," are worth noticing because of their fluently shifting scenes. The freedom in a radio script to shift scenes simply and easily may well have had some bearing on much of Miller's later work, such as *Death of a Salesman*, *A View from the Bridge*, and *After the Fall*. Despite the realistic manner of *The Man Who Had All the Luck*, *All My Sons*, and *The Crucible*, Miller has never regarded realism as an end in itself, but only as a tool to be mastered.

The radio plays may have had another influence on the development of Miller's mature technique. Two of these plays are stories told by a narrator and one of them concludes with a scene in Heaven. In his mature plays, Miller has been absorbed by the problems that Ibsenian realism did not quite satisfactorily solve. These are the problems of how to range more broadly through time and of how to probe more deeply into the mind than the front-parlor drama allows. Without wishing to curtail the objectivity of realism, he has wanted to combine with it some of the subjective strength to be found in various nonrealistic manners like that of the dream play or expressionism. As he wrote in "On Social Plays," the struggle taking place in the drama today is "a struggle at one and the same time to write of private persons privately and yet lift up their means of expression to a poetic — that is, a social — level." His most effective way so far of solving this problem is by the technique of the narrator which he first used in these early radio plays.

Having made something of a reputation by his radio work, Miller was hired in 1944 by Lester Cowan, a movie producer, to visit army camps and gather material for *The Story of GI Joe*, a film to be based more or less on Ernie Pyle's newspaper columns. He spent a couple of months at army camps, observing various types of training, and talking with officers and men. What came out of the experience was his book of reportage, *Situation Normal*. The book is still worth reading, although not so much for its rather superficial reporting as for a pervasive idealism which Miller would probably now consider naive. Actually, the book sheds more light on Miller the writer than on the war and the army.

His producer had commissioned him to find out what the war and the army were really like, so that this film would be an honest one that avoided the usual cinema clichés. To this purpose, Miller added another, for "you cannot," he wrote, "make a true picture of this war until you make up your mind as to what this war is about." Actually, the book makes clear that Miller had already decided what the war was about and that he was really attempting to discover his conclusions in the men he talked to. His attempts to draw generalizations from the soldiers about the nature of fascism and democracy came to nothing, however, and even in his discussions with Ernie Pyle he did not find this broad concern with the reasons for the war. He wrote: "It is terrible to me that everything is so personal; I mean that never in any of these calculations about the soldier can I honestly bring in the socio-political context of this war. I can't seem to find men who betray a social responsibility as a reason for doing or not doing anything. Maybe it was always so. Maybe that's why Tom Paine got drunk all the time." He was too honest a reporter to describe what he did not see, but he was also too committed a thinker to relinquish his preconceptions. "I can't give up the idea that political and economic beliefs have something to do with how these men react to this training and to the idea of fighting." Perhaps, he thought, the soldiers did have the beliefs for which he was searching, even though "in a totally unsuspected guise, in different forms than writers usually conceive them . . . through some osmotic absorption."

To oversimplify Miller's view somewhat, he regarded the war as a struggle between the principles of democratic equality and fascistic tyranny, and his book shows him determined to discover this same view in men for whom it was a purely academic and even an irrelevant point. His book makes quite clear that this view, even though he did not find it in the soldiers, is still going to be the focal point of the film which is jelling in his mind. In other words, Miller is attempting in this first book exactly what he would attempt again and again in his mature plays — to give to individual man, from the workings of society, his reason for existence, his personal significance, and his morality. Here his quest seems quixotic, for, although there were broad, underlying political and economic reasons for the war, those reasons had little connection with the individual soldier. In *Situation Normal* Miller is rationalizing, almost creating the connection. In his subsequent work up to *The Misfits*, he continued to search for connections. To an extent with *The Misfits* and almost totally with *After the Fall*, Miller seems to have given up the search, so actually one might read his career to date as a growing disillusionment with social idealism.

Miller had his first professional production of a play when *The Man Who Had All the Luck* appeared on Broadway on November 23, 1944, and lasted for four performances. The play gives the impression of being almost a student exercise. To paraphrase Willy Loman, it seems contrived, but not well contrived. The crucial situation at the end of the last act is strong, but artificial, a theatrically constructed situation rather than a real and inevitable one. Indeed, the drama throughout is a kind of poorly made well-made play that progresses through a series of climaxes to the greatest climax. Nevertheless, it is more loosely structured than an Ibsen play. It is spread over four years rather than a few days, and the entire story is dramatized rather than merely the events immediately preceding the climax. The characters are clearly drawn, but some are purely illustrative and are dropped when their purpose is served, rather than being meaningfully interwoven throughout the story. All of the characters seem fugitives from a regional folk drama, and this tendency is especially noticeable in the first act. Perhaps the point might be made clear just by listing some of their names — J. B. Feller, Amos Beeves, Hester Falk, Dan Dibble.

The strength of the play is its emphasis upon moral responsibility, and that same emphasis would be the strength of Miller's mature work. The main character, David Frieber, or David Beeves as he was called in the produced version, feels guilty for having been successful without real merit or effort. He feels destined to pay for his good luck by the stillbirth of his child. If his child's death makes up for his unmerited good luck, he can then, he feels, sink all of his efforts into raising mink and can succeed for once by his own abilities. When the child is born perfectly healthy, David becomes obsessed by his need for success until his wife forces him to let the mink die, although the death of the animals will wipe away most of their prosperity.

Several themes touched vaguely upon in this play become the clearly enunciated ones of *All My Sons* and *Death of a Salesman* — the themes, for instance, of money and morality and of individual responsibility. Here, however, individual responsibility is not really connected to man's social responsibility. The play is set in no really believable background, but is a kind of disengaged moral fable about a particular individual. To the mature play-wright, that fact would seem a major fault.

In writing the play, Miller had tried, he remarked, "to grasp wonder, I had tried to make it on the stage, by writing wonder. But wonder had betrayed me and the only other course I had was the one I took — to seek cause and effect, hard actions, facts, the geometry of relationships, and to hold back any tendency to express an idea in itself unless it was literally forced out of a character's mouth; in other words, to let wonder rise up like a mist, a gas, a vapor from the gradual and remorseless crush of factual and psychological conflict."

To solve this problem, Miller returned to *The Brothers Kara-mazov*, and found "that if one reads its most colorful, breath-taking, wonderful pages, one finds the thickest concentration of hard facts." He also decided that "the precise collision of inner themes" must occur "during, not before or after, the high dramat-ic scenes," and that the climax must be held back and back until the themes were properly clear. In other words, he came closer to the austere Ibsenian tragedy whose chief components were a meticulously drawn, real society, a tightly constructed cumulative structure, and an overwhelming insistence on significant theme.

The other pertinent point about the play is that Miller learned from it that his themes must be ones which deeply, personally in-volved him. Puzzling over the faults of the play, he found that ". . . two of the characters, who had been friends in the previous drafts, were logically brothers and had the same father. Had I known then what I know now I could have saved myself a lot of trouble. The play was impossible to fix because the overt story was only tangential to the secret drama its author was quite un-consciously trying to write. But in writing of the father-son rela-tionship and of the son's search for his relatedness there was a fullness of feeling I had never known before; a crescendo was struck with a force I could almost touch. The crux of *All My Sons*, which would not be written until nearly three years later, was formed; and the roots of *Death of a Salesman* were sprouted." With this discovery Miller found himself. In his best known plays, as in perhaps the best dramas of the Western world, the larger society is reflected by the little society of the family. That little society, that microcosm, Miller knew intimately and revealingly documented.

Although Miller is primarily a playwright, he has written a novel and several short stories. His novel *Focus*, published in 1945, was generally well received and sold about 90,000 copies in its hard-cover edition. The specific subject of the book is anti-Semitism, but its more general concern is that irrational hatred directed toward practically any racial minority.

The story charts the social education of Lawrence Newman, an easygoing Gentile with a vague, casual prejudice against Jews. When a new pair of glasses makes him appear Jewish, he is demoted from his job. Affronted, Newman resigns, but is unable to get his particular kind of job elsewhere because other people now also take him for a Jew. When his neighbors form a Christian Front to run a small Jewish merchant out of the neighborhood, Newman is apathetic about joining, and his actions make the others so suspicious that he is also taken by them as a Jew. Newman himself recognizes no kinship with Mr. Finkelstein the merchant and advises him for his own safety to leave the neighborhood. Newman refuses to leave because he regards his own case as different. No matter what the Christian Front thinks, he is really a Gentile. It is not until he is set upon by a group of toughs and with Finkelstein fights them off with baseball bats that he realizes his actual kinship. When he reports the attack, he allows the police to consider him a

Jew, thus admitting to himself not so much Jewishness as something broader, the brotherhood of man.

The theme is strongly stated, and the book remains engrossing despite its quite fuzzily drawn background. A more damaging fault is the unconvincing change in Newman. It is quite conceivable that, under the pressure of the story's events, a man would change from apathy to involvement. But Newman in the beginning of the story is pictured as a flabby, middle-aged Prufrock; in the middle he for no convincing reason attracts and marries a beautiful woman; by the end he is almost a hero of popular melodrama, athletically repelling assailants with his baseball bat.

In the smaller matters of Newman's changing character, Miller is more successful — for instance, when Newman, conscious of appearing Jewish, represses his usual gestures, refuses to count his change, and overtips the waitress. In the difficult larger task of showing how a man's character changes when his face changes, Miller is less convincing. The fault does not detract from the force of the book's point, but it does from its value as a work of art. It is a book of the moment, no worse than Laura Z. Hobson's *Gentleman's Agreement*, but no better either.

Miller's first really accomplished work was the play *All My Sons*, which was produced on January 29, 1947, and had a Broadway run of 328 performances. The play established Miller as a dramatist of much promise and was given the Drama Critics Circle Award as the best American play of the season. That award was something of an overestimation, for the same season saw the first production of O'Neill's masterly *The Iceman Cometh*. Nevertheless, *All My Sons* is a strong, traditional well-made play whose technique insists upon comparison with the realistic plays of Ibsen. Like them, *All My Sons* begins almost immediately before the climax of its story. Most of the story has occurred before the curtain rises and is revealed by exposition subtly interwoven with the current action. Actually, this structure was not unique with Miller or Ibsen or even Racine. One may find precisely the same structure in *Oedipus Rex*; in Sophocles' play, as in Miller's, the revelation of a criminal whose crime has occurred years earlier is the crux of the present action. However, in Miller's play the Oedipus character is split in two — one half being the father and criminal and the other half the son and detective.

This structure is difficult to handle, for the playwright must explain rather than dramatize most of the action, and the great bulk of exposition always threatens to dissipate the dramatic impact of the play. There are probably three chief ways to combat this threat: by the evocative beauty of the dialogue, by irony, and by an adroit blending of current action with explanation of past action. In his *Oedipus Rex*, Sophocles superbly managed all three ways. In his social plays, Ibsen lacked poetry, but his permeating irony largely compensated for the realistic flatness of his style, and he did blend his past and present action with incomparable adroitness. In *All My Sons*, Miller handles his plot consummately, but he notably lacks both the poetry and the irony. Nevertheless, structure alone can carry a play very far, and Miller's play, because of its structure, remains absorbing theater.

It is the story of Joe Keller, a small manufacturer, who during the war allowed some faulty engine blocks to be shipped to the air force. When a number of planes crashed, Keller and his partner were brought to trial. Keller was finally released and his partner blamed, although Keller himself was really responsible. The theme, then, is one of morality and money, and the action centers around the attempt of Keller's son Chris to find the truth and to fix the responsibility, and of Keller to avoid his responsibility. The point of his guilt is only brought home to him after a letter is produced proving that his other son Larry had also considered his father guilty and had died in combat as a kind of expiation. Then Joe recognizes that the other pilots who died were "all my sons" and in expiation he kills himself.

This action does not at first dominate the play. It is brought to a head by the current action, a false plot which seems at the beginning to be the story's major substance. Chris has asked his brother's fiancée home because he intends to marry her. However, Chris's mother refuses to believe that Larry really died in battle, and much of the play's first two acts is an attempt to convince her, so that Chris and Ann may marry.

As in *Oedipus Rex* or *Ghosts*, the real plot emerges from the present action like a ghost from the past. It comes to dominate that action and to be the center of the play. This plot from the past, even in the beginning of the play, is constantly intruded; we are constantly reminded of Joe's trial and Larry's death. Such a technique may seem at first to slow the pace, until we see that it is revealing the real action. When such a parallel plot is well handled, there is a suspenseful tension as the relationship between past and present becomes ever clearer.

Like Ibsen's social plays, Miller's play is economical. All of his characters, even the minor ones, have an integral relation to the theme. No characters are introduced merely to illustrate or to facilitate the mechanics of the plot. Such economy emphasizes the play's closeness to traditional austere tragedy. This is a family tragedy; the father is a man of some importance who falls from power to ignominy. The lives of his entire family are blighted by his crime. Such a description might just as well apply to the royal family of Thebes or to the Alving family of Norway.

18

There is even in the play a hint of fate inexorably guiding the destinies of the characters. It is the ghost from the past, the dead son, whose words precipitate the tragic climax. In one of the minor characters who is preparing a horoscope of the dead son, the play even has a prophet. That last fact suggests the distance between the austere stylized tragedy of Sophocles and Racine and the austere realistic tragedy of Ibsen and Miller. Ibsen had attempted to inject the supernatural into some of his realistic dramas — such as, for instance, the white horses in *Rosmersholm.* Perhaps his intention was to compensate for a lack of grandeur and tragic import which might derive from realistic dialogue and a middle-class setting. Ibsen was not, however, entirely successful in bringing a sense of fate into the front parlor, and turned away in his last plays from the illusion of total realism. Miller's intrusion of the supernatural is even more apologetically introduced than Ibsen's white horses. Most of the characters discount the horoscope, and the audience takes Miller's prophet as a mildly comic relief in a basically serious play. Consequently, Miller loses even the small effect that Ibsen gained, and his play seems smaller.

That smallness is particularly evident in the play's conclusion. Toward the end of the last act, Miller increases the intensity of the action to an extent that seems overwrought and frenetic when compared to the ambling and realistic tone of the earlier part. There is in the theater, unless the play is done excellently, some incongruity, as if the ending of an Elizabethan blood tragedy had been attached to a play by Terence Rattigan.

Nevertheless, despite its lack of irony, of really composed dialogue, and of characters who live outside of a theater, *All My Sons* is a real accomplishment. Its characters, if somewhat flat, do not have the dishonest flatness of many stage characters. Its theme seems likely to remain deeply pertinent for American society, and it is a model of structural craftsmanship. Probably its excellences of theme and structure will keep it fresh for as long as those excellences kept green the plays of John Galsworthy. That is certainly a limited immortality, but scarcely a contemptible one.

The promise of *All My Sons* was more than fulfilled when *Death of a Salesman* was produced on Broadway on February 10, 1949, and ran for 742 performances. It was excitingly staged by Elia Kazan and given memorable performances by Mildred Dunnock, Arthur Kennedy, and the excellent Lee J. Cobb as Willy Loman. To many viewers the play seemed the most meaningful and moving statement made about American life upon the stage in a great many years, and it is still generally considered Miller's masterpiece. The play was awarded the Pulitzer Prize for drama, and solidified its author's reputation as a leading American dramatist and one of the country's significant writers.

Willy Loman, the salesman of the title, is like Joe Keller a typical embodiment of the modern business morality, but he is also a more universal figure. One feels that Joe Keller's individual story points up a valid flaw in the American dream, but that Willy's story is larger than one man's. Like even the great tragic figures of Sophocles and Shakespeare, Miller's Willy is both an individual and a broadly relevant type.

It is difficult to say what makes a character attain this rare meaningfulness. Perhaps Willy's universal quality stems, paradoxically, from his well-developed individuality. Certainly his broad meaningfulness partly stems from the compassion with which he is presented. With all of his faults — his weakness, his density, his petty irritations and self-delusions — this compassion yet remains dominant in the mind of the audience. Perceptive people probably consider that their own characters are similar compounds of weakness, delusion, and folly, but each man recognizes in himself, beneath his weight of self-criticism, an alleviating quality, a basic humanity. Whatever he has done, he at least meant well. This fact does not atone for his faults, but it is the extenuating circumstance that finally liberates Orestes and Hamlet and, in the Christian story, the sons of Adam. Miller has touched here a central chord in his view of Willy, and, except for *A Memory of Two Mondays*, he has not been interested in touching it again. That fact probably explains why *Death of a Salesman* has moved audiences more deeply than Miller's other work. All of his plays are condemnations of human nature, but *Death of a Salesman* condemns with pity and sorrow.

More generally considered, Willy is the modern man who has accepted wholeheartedly the twentieth-century version of the American dream, and who then reacts like the psychologist's rat when it discovers that the door to its particular dream has been inexplicably shut. Willy has swallowed the modern version of the Horatio Alger myth, that unrealistic notion that if you are a clean-living and diligent bank clerk you will marry the boss's daughter and become chairman of the board. Whatever its flaws, this male Cinderella story had some admirable qualities. It approved of honesty, industry, and thrift, and so it was not quite the view that you would get something for nothing. Its modern version has become debased, and is dangerously close to the view that you will get something for nothing. Willy has applied himself; he has been diligent and thrifty; he has extolled the businessman's virtues; he has tried to be "well-liked." For this he should have been rewarded, but no reward comes, and Willy is numbly baffled by the failure of the American dream.

Willy's story points up how the Alger story and, presumably, the national morality have become tarnished. To the Alger hero, there was no discrepancy between his ideals and his life.

In Willy's time, there is a double standard, and he is not entirely aware of it. While preaching to his sons clean living, friendliness, sportsmanship, and honesty, his life denies these qualities. He has a mistress on the road, his friendliness does not really sell merchandise, and it dimly occurs to him that people don't really consider it even friendliness. His son Biff, the star athlete in high school, does not finally win out over Bernard the greasy grind, and Willy's values do not lead to success and happiness. A basic tolerance for dishonesty permeates his actions, and this dishonesty is reflected in the lives of his sons.

Nevertheless, in their broadest sense, Willy's hopes and goals were pure, and pity and sorrow arise for his agony when he does not attain them. Like Oedipus, Willy Loman made the wrong choice. He hitched his wagon to the wrong star. We can feel pity and sorrow for his mistake rather than contempt, for, after all, he was searching for a star.

The language of the play is much better than that of *All My Sons*. It contains some of the tragicomic irony that Ibsen used so effectively in his social plays. For instance, Willy remarks: "Oh, I'll knock 'em dead next week. I'll go to Hartford. I'm very well liked in Hartford. You know, the trouble is, Linda, people don't seem to take to me." Or:

WILLY: Chevrolet, Linda, is the greatest car ever built. . . .

LINDA: . . . you owe Frank for the carburetor.

WILLY: I'm not going to pay that man! That goddam Chevrolet, they ought to prohibit the manufacture of that car!

Such touches are not as pervasive as in Ibsen, but there are enough to suggest a fuller, more anguished, more pathetic, and more contradictory humanity than Miller had presented in *All My Sons*.

Another ironic device contributing to the fullness of Willy's character is the exaggerated speech which the audience but not the speaker realizes is too farfetched to come true. Each of the Lomans has such speeches, but the most and the finest are Willy's. For instance: "You and Hap and I, and I'll show you all the towns. America is full of beautiful towns and fine, upstanding people. And they know me, boys, they know me up and down New England. The finest people. And when I bring you fellas up, there'll be open sesame for all of us, 'cause one thing, boys: I have friends. I can park my car in any street in New England, and the cops protect it like their own."

The play is a notable technical achievement, for in it Miller broke out of the realistic confinements of time and space and psychology. At one time he called the play *Inside His Mind*, and much of the play is sieved through Willy's eyes. The viewpoint is not quite constant, and it is a little difficult to tell from what viewpoint some of the scenes should be seen. However, as there should be no confusion in production about the point of any of the scenes, the question of who technically is the narrator is somewhat academic.

In theme and technique, the play accomplishes exactly what Miller wanted. It is not confined to Ibsen's front parlor or to the few hours preceding the climax nor do we have to interpret what a person feels merely from what he says. The play beautifully balances the interior of a man's mind with a full evocation of his world. By his own standards, Miller had succeeded, and his standards in this instance coincided with everyone else's.

Miller's adaptation of Ibsen's *An Enemy of the People* was produced on Broadway on December 28, 1950, but, despite a cast headed by Fredric March, Florence Eldridge, and Morris Carnovsky, it lasted only 36 performances. Although not an eloquent play, Miller's version is fluent and streamlined. The stiff and old-fashioned flavor of the Archer translation is far from Miller's mid-century Americanese which strikes the ear as both colloquial and easy. Many of Ibsen's long expositions and tirades are drastically reduced, so that the adaptation is only about two-thirds the length of the original. Ibsen had a tendency to lengthen, sometimes almost interminably, the action following the climax, and Miller's abridgement of the last act makes the play more emphatic to modern ears than Ibsen's leisurely recapitulation of each dramatic point. The other main abridgement is in the meeting scene which Miller may have pared down too much. His cutting swiftens and heightens the action, but probably loses some of the rhetorical force of Ibsen's long speeches.

Miller made three other notable changes. He made the play from a five-act one into a three-act and five-scene one. He made the curtains more theatrically effective, and, although he has opposed theatrical effect for its own sake, Miller does not despise it when it rises honestly out of the action. Finally, Ibsen tended to write set scenes in the French style, each scene existing in its separate compartment and a set of new characters being introduced for each succeeding scene. Miller runs many of these scenes into each other and eliminates or smooths over the transitions between them. Such tinkering could not be entirely successful without violently wrenching Ibsen's structure, but Miller does reduce the — to modern taste — tight artificiality which Ibsen inherited from the well-made play.

More interesting than Miller's innovations in Ibsen's script is his choice of this particular play and the light that his choice throws upon his own work. Reading Ibsen was for Miller almost as crucial as reading Dostoevski. Of course, Ibsen's obvious influence, particularly if one thinks of *All My Sons* or *The Crucible*, was for a firmly wrought form and structure. Miller has spoken almost in the same breath of the "enthralling dramatic experience of reading Ibsen" and of his dissatisfaction with formless "slapped together" plays like Michael V. Gazzo's *A*

Hatful of Rain. Nevertheless, for Miller as well as for Shaw, technique was not the ultimate lesson to be learned from Ibsen. Ibsen's real strength and importance to Miller is " . . . his insistence, his utter conviction, that he is going to say what he has to say, and that the audience, by God, is going to listen. . . . Every Ibsen play begins with the unwritten words: 'Now listen here!' And these words have shown me a path through the wall of 'entertainment,' a path that leads beyond the formulas and dried-up precepts, the pretense and fraud, of the business of the stage. Whatever else Ibsen has to teach, this is his first and greatest contribution." In other words, "Attention must be paid," and a serious play achieves its drama primarily from its content rather than from its emotional effects. This point, that a play must be a significant statement, is Ibsen's chief legacy to the modern playwright and the chief reason why Arthur Miller is one of the sons of Henrik.

The reason for Miller's adapting this particular play, which is not one of Ibsen's great achievements, throws much light on Miller's own preoccupations. He remarked in his preface to the play that its theme was "the central theme of our social life today. Simply, it is the question of whether the democratic guarantees protecting political minorities ought to be set aside in time of crisis. More personally, it is the question of whether one's vision of the truth ought to be a source of guilt at a time when the mass of men condemn it as a dangerous and devilish lie." This same view impelled the writing of *The Crucible* and this same problem Miller himself had to face six years later when he was called to appear before the House Committee on Un-American Activities. This play suggests the answer that, when the times are out of joint, the individual must to himself be true. Stockmann, as Miller puts it, "clings to the truth and suffers the social consequences. At rock bottom, then, the play is concerned with the inviolability of objective truth. Or, put more dynamically, that those who attempt to warp the truth for ulterior purposes must inevitably become warped and corrupted themselves."

This conclusion about the corruption of society is a distinct change from the premise of *Situation Normal* and *All My Sons*, which suggested that society is the giver of morality and that man succeeds or fails by his ability to find a home in that society. It is a conclusion which apparently Miller sought to avoid and which he accepted only after much struggle. In the 1940's his view was one of a simple social idealism, and the issues were clear-cut. As Quentin remarks in *After the Fall*: ". . . the world [was] so wonderfully threatened by injustices I was born to correct! How fine! Remember? When there were good people and bad people? And how easy it was to tell! The worst son of a bitch, if he loved Jews and Negroes and hated Hitler — he was a buddy. Like some kind of paradise compared to this." However, Miller was too perceptive a man not to be moved by the nature of his society, and it seemed to him that that society was growing more and more malevolent. Consequently, we find a confusion in his writing; we find succeeding works contradicting the previous ones. *Situation Normal* applauded society, but *Focus* condemned it. *All My Sons* applauded society, but *Death of a Salesman* and *The Crucible* condemned it. *A View from the Bridge* applauded society, but *A Memory of Two Mondays* condemned it. In other words, much of Miller's work does not derive from inalterable conviction, but from a conflict of two opposed convictions.

That conflict appears clearly in his adaptation of Ibsen. In Ibsen's crucial fourth scene, Dr. Stockmann is pushed to defend a biological aristocracy of superior men, like the Superman of Nietzsche. This concept is an almost inevitable conclusion of the fierce condemnation of society that grows out of the play's action, but it is not a point that the perplexed Miller was yet willing to admit. He therefore eliminated this speech from the play. Much of Miller's work up to *The Misfits* is centered around this conflict between the ideal and the real. Some of his plays expressed one view, some the other, but he was being increasingly pushed in one direction, and by *The Misfits* he had made his mind up.

Miller is a slow, painstaking, and deliberate writer who sometimes composes thousands of pages to get a hundred that are right. Consequently, his next original play, *The Crucible*, did not appear until January 22, 1953. It was generally thought a sound work but a lesser one than *Death of a Salesman*. In its original run it achieved only 197 performances, but its off-Broadway revival several years later played well over 500. Its merits were at first overshadowed by the notoriety of its most obvious theme. The subject of the play, the Salem witch trials of 1692, was distractingly applicable to what has been called the witch hunts of the 1950's. Now, when the most impassioned fervor of Communist hunting has abated, the play may probably be judged on its own merits, unobscured by newspaper headlines.

The Crucible is a strong play, and its conclusion has much of the force of tragedy. It has not the permeating compassion of *Death of a Salesman*, but there is more dramatic power to John Proctor's death than there was to Willy's. It is a harder hitting play, and its impact stems from Proctor's death being really a triumph. You cannot pity a man who triumphs. Willy Loman's death was a failure, and his suicide only a gesture of defeat. Him you can pity.

The Crucible is really a more dramatic play than *Death of a Salesman*. The earlier play attempted to construct a plot about Willy's losing his job, and Biff's attempting to gain one, but these strands of plot were only a frame on which to hang the exposition of a man's whole life. The plots of *Death of a Salesman* are not the center of the play, but in *The Crucible* the action is the play's very basis, its consuming center. One watches *Death of a Salesman* to discover what a man is like, but one watches *The Crucible* to discover what a man does. *Death of a Salesman* is a tour de force that succeeds despite its slim action because its real center is the accumulation of enough significant detail to suggest a man. In the life of John Proctor, one single action is decisive, dominating, and totally pertinent, and this action, this moment of decision and commitment, is that climax toward which every incident in the play tends. *Death of a Salesman* is not traditionally dramatic, at least in the Aristotelian sense that the center of a drama is an action. *The Crucible* is so dramatic, and the centrality of its plot explains its greater strength.

That strength is also explained by the clarity with which the theme of *The Crucible* emerges from its plot. The theme of *Death of a Salesman* does not emerge so much from its story as from its illustration and exposition. For that reason it is necessary for Linda and Charley in their laments to explain the meaning of Willy's life, and actually Linda is still explaining what the play means in the last scene. *The Crucible* requires no such exposition, for the play's meaning has been acutely dramatized. The exposition in *Death of a Salesman* is dramatic only in the way that the keening in *Riders to the Sea* is dramatic. It is a lyrical evocation of emotion rather than a dramatic one.

The Crucible is more traditionally dramatic in one other way. The theme of a play is made more intense by the hero's either making a discovery of past folly (Oedipus, Lear) or being presented with an agonizing dilemma (Orestes, Hamlet). Proctor's story has elements of both situations. His past folly, which he has been trying unsuccessfully to live down, is his seduction of Abigail Williams, and this fault eventually destroys him when Abigail turns against him and accuses him of witchcraft. The center of the play, however, is his dilemma about commitment. This dilemma is stated in each act in somewhat different terms. In Act I, Proctor washes his hands of the town's problem and refuses to be involved in the absurd charges of witchcraft being made by a small group of frightened, hysterical girls. In Act II, he is pushed into involvement when Abigail denounces his wife Elizabeth as a witch. In Act III, he attempts legally to rescue the accused, but by resorting to law also attempts to avoid being involved himself. Finally, at the end of the act, he can only achieve justice by involvement, and so he accuses Abigail and becomes himself one of the accused. Proctor's identification with the accused is not yet total. He drags his feet as did Lawrence Newman. He suffers with them for months in prison, but in the final moment before his execution he signs a confession of witchcraft. His reason is that he is really different from them. He cries: "I cannot mount the gibbet like a saint. It is a fraud. I am not that man. My honesty is broke, Elizabeth; I am no good man. Nothing's spoiled by giving them this lie that were not rotten long before." Proctor is still striving for a compromise, but Miller will allow him none. Proctor signs the confession to save his life, but the judges demand that the confession be made public, and he finds that he cannot live in society uncommitted. He must be either totally and publicly against the accused or totally and publicly with them. There is no middle ground of private commitment and public neutrality. This is Proctor's final dilemma as it was Lawrence Newman's and Joe Keller's, and Miller will not, at this point in his career, allow the individual to escape from his social obligation into his private life.

Two points connect this situation with the tradition of austere tragedy. First, an individual is pushed to definition, forced to irreclaimable and self-destructive action. That self-destruction is, paradoxically, an affirmation of morality, for it asserts that belief is more important than life. Second, the individual discovers his need to choose, and his agony comes from his awareness. Reason, said Milton, is but choosing, and Proctor's aware choice is the choice of a reasoning man. That last point indicates the distance between Proctor's tragedy and Willy Loman's. Willy's is a kind of passive, uncomprehending, mute, brute suffering. Whatever peace Willy attains by his death is the peace of oblivion, but whatever peace Proctor attains is the peace of knowledge. Willy's is a pathetic tragedy, Proctor's an austere one. Willy's story arouses pity, Proctor's suffering. Willy's death is a lament for the destruction of value, Proctor's a paean to its creation. And finally, Willy's is the story of man's failure, and Proctor's the story of man's triumph.

Technically the play is not as interesting as *Death of a Salesman* or as tightly structured as *All My Sons*. Its structure is, however, appropriate for the retelling of the witch hunt story and for the revelation to Proctor of the need for commitment. Its language is not as lyrically evocative as that of *Death of a Salesman*, but it does not need to be. In *Death of a Salesman* language had to be a substitute for plot; here it can be unobtrusively subservient. Actually the dialogue of the play is a considerable accomplishment. It suggests the flavor of seventeenth-century speech without becoming distractingly archaic and without sacrificing simplicity, strength, or suppleness.

Death of a Salesman may always be considered a better play than *The Crucible* for two reasons. First, there were no distracting headlines to hurt the initial impact of the earlier play, and the American theater is so commercially and journalistically oriented that even a later success can rarely erase the first impression. Second, and even more important, the emotions evoked by the pathetic tragedy are closer to the surface than those aroused by the austere one. Hamlet is a fuller and more intelligent view of humanity than is Cyrano and Proctor than Willy, but they will never arouse as many tears. The fault is not in the playwright but in the naiveté of his form, and the naiveté of his form is dictated by the naiveté of his audience — in other words, by human nature.

Two and a half years later, on September 29, 1955, Miller had produced on Broadway two one-act plays, *A Memory of Two Mondays* and *A View from the Bridge*. The production was not entirely happy, and the plays closed after a moderate run of 149 performances. Later Miller revised and expanded *A View from the Bridge* into two acts, and its subsequent London production achieved considerable success.

On the plays' first production, most of the critics paid little or no attention to *A Memory of Two Mondays*. However, one of the most astute critics, the canny Irishman Frank O'Connor, thought it the better play, and Miller himself remarked in the Introduction to his *Collected Plays* that "Nothing in this book was written with greater love, and for myself I love nothing printed here better than this play."

One of the clichés about Miller is that he has no humor. There is really a great deal of humor in his work, and in no place is it more theatrically effective than in this superb little tragicomedy. Miller himself calls the play "a pathetic comedy," and it would be hairsplitting to quarrel with his definition. There is more of pathos than of tragedy in the play, and one of its main effects is the pity evoked for the people who stay on in the automobile parts warehouse after Bert leaves to go to college. Even so, the play has some effects stronger than pathos.

31

The old, hardy, ribald Gus, impelled to carouse all weekend because of twenty-two years of accumulated monotony from the warehouse, yet obsessed with guilt for having been carousing when his wife was dying, awakens an emotion stronger than pity. He first lugs two Ford automobile fenders around all weekend. Then he draws all of his money from the bank and goes on a last great spree, buys a suit of clothes, rents three taxis simultaneously, drinks, calls all of his friends long-distance, and finally dies in one of his taxis. Automobiles were the cross of Gus's life, but he did die with some heroic bravado. Gus's life just as fully squashes him as Willy Loman's did to him, but he is more than a low man or a new man or a GI Joe killer. He has also his load of guilt, but he has a vigor about him, an indomitability.

This play is a considerable achievement. Tragicomedy requires that the stories of a number of people be told. It requires that not merely one mood, but various conflicting ones be evoked. It usually requires irony and it often uses lyricism and song. These qualities are all present in Miller's play, and it is remarkable that he was able to pack so much in so effectively. In a way it is like trying to pack *The Plough and the Stars* into one act and succeeding. This is a moving, technically adroit, and beautiful job, one of the rare instances of a one-act tragicomedy.

Miller's descent from the austere tragic writers is nowhere more evident than in the first version of *A View from the Bridge*. That play seems an attempt to utilize the austere technique of Sophocles in a modern setting, just as Maxwell Anderson's *Winterset* was an attempt to do the same thing with the manner of Shakespeare. Miller's first version uses the sparest outline of the traditional tragic plot, a typical tragic situation, and a chorus, and it is written in what might be tolerantly called free verse. Its traditional austerity is discussed by Miller in his essay "On Social Plays" where he remarks: "*A View from the Bridge* is in one act because . . . these *qualities* of the events themselves, their texture, seemed to me more psychologically telling than a conventional investigation in width which would necessarily relax that clear, clean line of his catastrophe." The story is about Eddie Carbone, a longshoreman in Brooklyn, who has raised his niece Catherine from a child. Now that she is older, he is reluctant to let her go. Eddie and his wife Beatrice take in two Italian relatives, Marco and Rodolpho, who have entered the country illegally to find work. When Catherine and Rodolpho fall in love, Eddie becomes desperate in his attempts to hold onto the girl's affections, and he finally turns the men in to the immigration officials. Denounced to the neighborhood by Marco, Eddie denies his guilt, and when the two men fight Eddie is killed.

The play is strongly effective on the stage, yet, except in the broadest sense as a story of a man driven by a secret passion, it probably has a lesser relevance than do the stories of Joe Keller or Willy Loman. Like Willy, Eddie does not fully understand or at least admit the force that is destroying him, and like John Proctor Eddie is ultimately concerned with saving his name. At the climactic moments of both *The Crucible* and *A View from the Bridge*, the protagonist is destroyed by his need to secure a place in society. In all of Miller's plays up to this time, morality is established by the society. In *Death of a Salesman* and *The Crucible* the morality is false; in *All My Sons* and *A View from the Bridge* it is valid. Up to this last play, Miller still saw the establishment of a social morality as the way out of the impasse of studies of individual disintegration which formed, he thought, the subjects of the bulk of serious drama and fiction in modern times. However, there are two social moralities in this play — the valid one which proves Eddie morally wrong for denouncing the illegal immigrants and which is held by the people, and the legal morality which no one believes in. The recognition of two social moralities is really a step away from the view of *All My Sons*, as well as another indication that Miller's work so far was in the nature of an interim report from a mind still irresolute.

A View from the Bridge, like *The Crucible*, has seemed a cold play, and actually Miller's only warm plays have been *Death of a Salesman* and *A Memory of Two Mondays*. Here, Miller's impatience with realism led him to draw a sparer protagonist than he had before, but the real coldness stems not from the relative lack of detail about Eddie, but from the artist's detachment from him. Miller has frequently gone on record as being opposed to plays which aim for easy theatrical effect rather than for significant point. His point is clearly made in *A View from the Bridge*, but the many touches of pervasive sympathy that made Willy Loman and Gus humanly relevant are missing. As Miller wrote in his Introduction to the revised version of the play: "It seemed to me then that the theater was retreating into an area of psycho-sexual romanticism, and this at the very moment when great events both at home and abroad cried out for recognition and analytic inspection. In a word, I was tired of mere sympathy in the theater. The spectacle of still another misunderstood victim left me impatient. The tender emotions, I felt, were being overworked. I wanted to write in a way that would call up the faculties of knowing as well as feeling." The revision of the play made Eddie theatrically somewhat fuller, but, as Miller remarked, "Eddie is still not a man to weep over; the play does not attempt to swamp an audience in tears." Whether an audience will allow such a play to succeed on its own grounds is still debatable. Racine and Ibsen succeeded, but in our own time the two authors who have most brilliantly striven to widen the intellectual content of a play, Bernard Shaw and Bertolt Brecht, have notably failed. Audiences frequently laugh at Shaw's jokes and forget or ignore what the jokes were about, and audiences at Brecht's *Mother Courage* insist on reading pathos into a place where the author wanted point.

In the theater, Miller's revision is not quite a total success. Eddie becomes fuller and Beatrice is drawn more into the action, but the theatrical quality of the earlier version is toned down. The lyric speeches of the lawyer Mr. Alfieri who acts as a kind of chorus are made shorter, more prosaic, and less theatrical. The climactic scene is toned down, and the fight between Marco and Eddie is shorter and less dramatic. When Eddie is stabbed he does not crawl across the stage and grasp Catherine's leg before he dies; rather, he dies in Beatrice's arms. This reconciliation with his wife perhaps normalizes Eddie more, but it also lessens his stature.

The impulse behind the play is commendable testimony to Miller's attempt to write meaningfully rather than to accept easy emotional effects and oversimple theatrical issues. Whether he can dispense with the easy emotional effect and force an austere and intellectual drama upon the modern stage is highly debatable. Foremost among the earlier American dramatists who wanted to make the drama a forum for intelligent discussion is Elmer Rice. Nevertheless in an introduction to two of his most intelligent and least successful plays, Rice held that a full and significant statement in a play was a contradiction and an impossibility, and that the drama demands that point be simplified and reduced to the usual theatrical tales of love and murder. Whether this view is ultimately true will not depend upon the Ibsens, Shaws, Rices, Brechts, and Millers of the modern drama who have tried to refute it, but upon the growth to maturity of the audience.

There followed a long hiatus in Miller's work for the stage that may be traced in part to his personal life and in part to his politics. Several of his plays had been attacked by organizations of the far right for their alleged Communist leanings (the same plays had run into trouble in Russia because of their alleged capitalist leanings), but his trouble with his own government really began when the State Department in 1954 refused him a passport "as a person believed to be supporting the Communist movement." His name was blackened somewhat more in 1955 when he was preparing a film scenario about the work of the New York Youth Board with juvenile delinquents. The American Legion and the Catholic War Veterans so strenuously objected to Miller on the basis of his alleged Communist sympathies that the film was ultimately dropped.

On June 21, 1956, Miller appeared before the House Committee on Un-American Activities and talked freely about his support of various Communist Front groups in the 1940's, and of how he had attended some Communist-sponsored meetings of writers. All questions about himself he answered fully and frankly, but he refused to answer two questions requiring him to name people whom he had seen at the meetings. For his refusal to name names, he was cited for contempt of Congress, fined $500, and given a suspended sentence of thirty days in jail, but he was also given a passport valid for six months.

The case was widely covered in the press because of Miller's eminence as a writer and also because of a turn his personal life had taken. His marriage had been deteriorating for several years, and in 1956 he divorced his wife and married Marilyn Monroe, the film actress. At the time, it seemed rather as if Albert Einstein had married Gypsy Rose Lee, for Miller was considered, as most playwrights are not, an intellectual, and Miss Monroe seemed the apotheosis of the dumb blonde.

To judge by what clearly are portraits of her in the short story "Please Don't Kill Anything" and in *After the Fall,* as well as by many overt remarks, Miller saw in Miss Monroe a rare example of innocence in the modern world, and the growing disillusionment of his own thought certainly prompted him to grasp at innocence. His troubles with the government were ultimately settled and the contempt citation was reversed, but his marriage kept him in the limelight. During these years he wrote much but published little, and his marriage began to absorb ever more of his time. According to Maurice Zolotow, Miss Monroe's biographer, whose testimony is supported by some comments in *After the Fall,* she drew him more and more into her own career.

The main accomplishment of these years was the film *The Misfits* which began as a short story, became a novel, and then a film script, and was finally published as a kind of novelized film script. The film, which was in some ways a vehicle for Marilyn Monroe, was not enthusiastically received, even though it was directed by John Huston and had also in its cast Eli Wallach, Montgomery Clift, and Clark Gable. It was a good film, honestly observed and craftily put together, but despite the presence of Marilyn Monroe it was not a conventionally glamorous film and did not abound in the naive theatricalities which the cinema demands. Many of the best regarded films — even *The Birth of a Nation, Greed, Stagecoach, Citizen Kane, Casablanca* — will hardly stand up under a second viewing which thoughtfully regards their content and is not swept away by their excitement. *The Misfits* has less of such conventional excitement than many films, but would probably grow in meaning rather than diminish on a second viewing.

The story concerns three cowboys in the modern West who drift aimlessly through life, muttering in the teeth of the modern world, "it's better than wages." The central part of the story is a mustang hunt carried on by airplane and truck. The mustang herd is now almost as small as the few men who hunt them, and the reason for the hunt is the ignoble one of selling the animals for dog food. What was once "a good thing to do . . . a man's work," has somehow gone wrong. As the oldest cowboy, Gay, explains it to the girl Roslyn: "We start out doin' something, meaning no harm, something that's naturally in us to do. And somewhere down the line it gets changed around into something bad. Like dancin' in a night club. You started out just wanting to dance, didn't you? And little by little it turns out that people ain't interested in how good you dance, they're gawkin' at you with something altogether different in their minds. And they turn it sour, don't they? . . . This . . . this is how I dance, Roslyn. And if they made somethin' else out of it, well . . . I can't run the world any more than you could. I hunt these horses to keep myself free. That's all."

In other words, Miller was talking about the destruction of innocence, and this film was his strongest indictment so far of both society and the family. The society is tawdry and valueless, and the family itself has disintegrated. Guido's wife has died, Perce has run away from home, Gay's children avoid him, and Roslyn's marriage has broken up. An effective symbol of this disintegration is the half-finished house which Guido started and then abandoned. This house in the desert is the closest that Miller had yet come to portraying a wasteland world in which things fall apart and the center cannot hold. The only true relationships are those casually formed between wandering misfits who still snatch what brief joys they can in a world in which they are ever more anachronistic.

But, although this was Miller's grimmest statement so far, he does not in the film entirely face up to the implications of his indictment. His characters are, as they must be for a movie, quite simple, almost childlike. Also a resolution comes too easily. In some indefinable way by freeing the mustangs they had caught, they become absolved of the sin of the world, and they all, with the possible exception of Guido, recapture a kind of innocence. Perce returns home to his family, and Gay and Roslyn have each other. As the picture closes, they are talking about a home, raising a family, and making a new start.

The film is finally neither meaningful enough nor dramatic enough because its point needs to be explored more thoroughly than Miller can in a film. He is just not able to use enough words, and his ending seems therefore not much more than the traditional Hollywood ending of the banal clinch and the ride off into the sunset. To make it work, this theme needs more depth, more meaning poured into it. That meaning Miller would try to include in his next play, *After the Fall*, when his indictment would be not only of society and of the family but also of the individual. The real trouble with *The Misfits* is that it is a movie, and the real difference in theme between it and Miller's latest play is that there are still in the movie a few individuals who can attain honor and innocence.

In 1960, Miller and Miss Monroe found life together intolerable, and they divorced. In 1962, he married Ingeborg Morath, a photographer for Reuters, and completed a new play, *After the Fall*, which was the initial presentation of the Lincoln Center Repertory Company. The play was so obviously based on Miller's life that its true merits were at first difficult to see. The journalistic critics were generally impressed while the critics attached to little reviews tended to attack it with a curious vehemence. Although the more literary of the reviewers dis-

sented, most observers felt that the play was brilliantly staged by
Kazan and enacted by an accomplished cast, which was headed
by Jason Robards, Jr., and had Barbara Loden in the role that
approximated the character of the recently dead Marilyn Monroe.

After the Fall is very possibly a masterpiece, but its excellence
may not clearly emerge until the false glamour of its autobio-
graphical elements has dimmed with time and also until critics
cease to compare it with some more conventional play — even
if that play is *Death of a Salesman* itself. Miller's increasing
dislike of superficially aroused emotion on the stage has in this
play increased his emphasis upon the theme, and an inevitable
consequence is the diminution of emotional appeal. The same
phenomenon can be seen in Shaw whose plays have also been
criticized as being all head and no heart. One might question
whether this is a mature criticism and, indeed, whether the
conventional drama is a particularly mature art. There may well
be, as *After the Fall* and much of Shaw's own work seem to
suggest, a deeper layer of emotion, more pertinent and more in-
tegrally connected to self-knowledge.

At any rate, *After the Fall* is Miller's most intellectually prob-
ing play, and Quentin is a central character too complicated to
be summed up by simple reactions of love and pity. The play
tells what happens to a man after the loss of intellectual innocence, after his Fall. Simple views of morality have failed Quentin, and he has lost his innocence not only as an individual but
as a member of the family and a member of society as well. As
an individual he has seen the wreckage of two marriages. He has
seen the failure of love both in his own family and among his
friends, both in his own country and in the world. Almost every
person in this play betrays love. In Quentin's words, "I loved
them all, all! And gave them willingly to failure and to death
that I might live, as they gave me and gave each other, with a

word, a look, a truth, a lie — and all in love!" Each person in the play seems to so sacrifice others for his own survival that love is made a travesty. As Quentin viciously puts it when dissecting Maggie's thoughts: "And I am full of hatred, I, Maggie, the sweet lover of all life — I hate the world! . . . Hate women, hate men, hate all who will not grovel at my feet proclaiming my limitless love for ever and ever!"

This picture of the individual scrambling to his own survival over the corpses of love is shown again and again in the play: in Quentin's two marriages, in his grateful relief when his friend Lou dies and he can avoid involvement in Lou's problems, in his deserting his father to go to college, in his mother's betrayal of him as a boy, in her betrayal of his bankrupt father, in the decision of Quentin's friend Mickey to betray his friends to the House investigating committee — in instance after instance, the individual betrays love to save himself. All of Quentin's three women accuse him of self-absorption, and the accusation is a true one, but it is also true for every other character in the play, save perhaps Holga whom Quentin is thinking of marrying at the end of the play. Even Quentin's second marriage, which is analogous to Gay and Roslyn's love in *The Misfits*, is shown to be merely a delusion that innocence can be recaptured. It cannot, and Maggie and Quentin turn on each other, and in a ghastly scene he refuses to help her save her own life.

The failure of love in a broad social sense is symbolized by the Nazi concentration camp and by the guilt that Quentin feels for it. Miller makes what happened in the concentration camp a macrocosm of what the individual does to others. When Quentin asks Holga, "Do you ever feel when you come here . . . some vague . . . complicity?" she answers, "Quentin . . . no one they didn't kill can be innocent again." Further, Mickey's decision to name names before the House committee is both

41

a comment upon the moral failure of a society which asks the individual such a question, and an example of a futile attempt to recapture a lost innocence. That innocence is, however, forever gone.

In light of this triple condemnation of society, the family, and the individual, it is apparent that Miller feels the inadequacy of the view of his earlier work. If this condemnation were the entire theme of *After the Fall*, the play would be one of the blackest of our time. However, Holga, who goes with Quentin to see *The Magic Flute*, is the character who brings a kind of hope — a bleak hope to be sure, but the only kind that would not seem a shoddy theatrical trick after the fable of this play:

> HOLGA: I had the same dream each night — that I had a child; and even in the dream I saw that the child was my life; and it was an idiot. And I wept, and a hundred times I ran away, but each time I came back it had the same dreadful face. Until I thought, if I could kiss it, whatever in it was my own, perhaps I could rest. And I bent to its broken face, and it was horrible. . . . but I kissed it.
>
> QUENTIN: Does it still come back?
>
> HOLGA: At times. But it somehow has the virtue now . . . of being mine. I think one must finally take one's life in one's arms, Quentin.

You must, as Quentin screams to Maggie, "see your own hatred, and live!" The damned and blasted and fallen man does not live "in some garden of wax fruit and painted trees, that lie of Eden, but after, after the Fall, after many, many deaths. . . . And the wish to kill is never killed, but with some gift of courage one may look into its face when it appears, and with a stroke of love — as to an idiot in the house — forgive it; again and again . . . forever?"

This is a remarkable statement from a battered man, and Quentin's grasping at this scrap of tattered certainty is far, far from the young Communist sympathizer of the 1940's holding aloft his white and unsullied banner, or from the starry-eyed author of patriotic simplicities in *Situation Normal,* or from the simple affirmations and condemnations of *The Man Who Had All the Luck, All My Sons,* or even *Death of a Salesman.* It is a statement to file away with other hard-won, hard-boiled verities like Stephen Dedalus' courage to be wrong or Faulkner's "They will endure." It is not precisely a *Reader's Digest* kind of sentiment, but it is probably one of the few mature remarks ever made in an American play.

Technically the play is a brilliant accomplishment. In it Miller solves his perennial problem of how to retain sufficient real psychology and a full feel of the real world and at the same time to attain a free flow of time and to probe more deeply into a man's mind than conventional realism allows. This play manages all of these matters without falling into the pitfalls of extreme expressionism or of the Theater of the Absurd. The play is told to an invisible narrator who might be, as Miller remarks, Quentin's analyst or God, but who really is Quentin himself. The play is an examination of conscience, and it takes place — to use the title which Miller discarded for *Death of a Salesman* — Inside His Mind.

By suggesting the way a man thinks, Miller is able to probe in detail and in depth Quentin's life. The play unfolds not by logical progression, but seemingly at random. Quentin shies away from certain thoughts, proceeds by association, doubles back upon his own thoughts, and yet there is no feeling of random repetition, but of an ever-increasing significance. One device holding the play together is the irony of stray thoughts that flit momentarily across Quentin's mind. For instance, a frequent apparition is the figure of Louise, Quentin's first wife, playing solitaire, and this figure appears as a swift accusation of Quentin's self-absorption in scenes with, for instance, Maggie the second wife. Other figures — Holga, his mother, his young admirer Felice — also appear instantaneously, and their mere appearance makes what they stand for in Quentin's life comment ironically upon a different situation. Strindberg in his dream plays also probed fascinatingly into man's mind but less logically and probably too chaotically for the simple necessities of the drama. Inheriting Ibsen's feel for structure and for point, Miller arranges the Strindbergian situation into a kind of order. Probably the only other American who has so ambitiously attempted the same thing is O'Neill in that baffling and brilliant chaos of a play, *The Great God Brown*.

Despite the charge of coldness and despite Quentin's considerably lacking the stature of Hamlet, to whom he has been compared, there is much fine characterization in the play. Maggie is the best character that Miller has drawn or attempted to draw since Willy Loman, and the other characters are not stinted, for even some minor parts are theatrically meaty roles. In sum, *After the Fall* has not ultimately solved all of Miller's technical problems, and it has not, of course, ultimately answered the problems that have bedeviled him and his world. In the play, he has even condemned that world in terms blacker than he had ever used before, but he has also seemed to discover that the questions worth asking are more complex than he earlier knew.

On December 3, 1964, in its second season, the Lincoln Center Theater presented Miller's most recent play, *Incident at Vichy*. Set in a "place of detention" in Occupied France in 1942, the play traces the agonies of a group of prisoners who have just been arrested. In form the play is a piece of adroit but quite straightforward realism. In theme it is basically a simpler restatement of the theme of *After the Fall*: all men are guilty because all men are human. Had the play appeared before *After the Fall*, it would have seemed more impressive. Coming afterward, it marks — despite its strength and honesty — no advance for Miller as either a theatrical technician or a thinker.

The unusual quickness with which Miller composed the play does suggest that he needs his own stage to spur him into activity. Unfortunately, the widespread dissatisfaction with the Lincoln Center Theater's first two seasons caused Miller (along with the group's artistic directors) to sever connections with the company. Since then Miller's only public work has been the collection of short stories, many of them written years earlier, called *I Don't Need You Any More* (1967). Whether he can be lured back into the theater and whether he will continue the interesting developments of *After the Fall* are, of course, unanswerable questions. But of this much at least we can be sure: his own position in the drama of the twentieth century is both secure and high.

◄ Selected Bibliography

Principal Works of Arthur Miller

PLAYS AND BOOKS

"The Pussycat and the Expert Plumber Who Was a Man," in *100 Non-Royalty Radio Plays*, compiled by William Kozlenko. New York: Greenberg, 1941.

"William Ireland's Confession," in *100 Non-Royalty Radio Plays*, compiled by William Kozlenko. New York: Greenberg, 1941.

The Man Who Had All the Luck, in *Cross-Section, 1944*, edited by Edwin Seaver. New York: L. B. Fischer, 1944.

Situation Normal. New York: Reynal and Hitchcock, 1944.

Focus. New York: Reynal and Hitchcock, 1945.

"Grandpa and the Statue," in *Radio Drama in Action*, edited by Erik Barnouw. New York: Farrar and Rinehart, 1945.

"That They May Win," in *The Best One-Act Plays of 1944*, edited by Margaret Mayorga. New York: Dodd, Mead, 1945.

"The Story of Gus," in *Radio's Best Plays*, edited by Joseph Liss. New York: Greenberg, 1947.

All My Sons. New York: Reynal and Hitchcock, 1947.

Death of a Salesman. New York: Viking, 1949.

An Enemy of the People. New York: Viking, 1951. (Adaptation of Ibsen's play with a Preface).

The Crucible. New York: Viking, 1953. (This play was printed with an additional scene in *Theatre Arts* for October 1953).

A View from the Bridge. New York: Viking, 1955. (Contains also *A Memory of Two Mondays* and the important preface "On Social Plays." The revised version in two acts was first printed in *Collected Plays* and later, with a new Introduction, was reprinted alone. New York: Viking, 1960.)

Collected Plays. New York: Viking, 1957. (Contains *All My Sons, Death of a Salesman, The Crucible, A View from the Bridge* in its revised version, *A Memory of Two Mondays*, and an important fifty-page Introduction.)

The Misfits. New York: Viking, 1961.

After the Fall. New York: Viking, 1964.

Incident at Vichy. New York: Viking, 1965.

I Don't Need You Any More. New York: Viking, 1967.

ARTICLES AND STORIES

"It Takes a Thief," *Collier's*, 119:23, 75–76 (February 8, 1947). (Story.)

"Subsidized Theatre," *New York Times* (June 22, 1947), Sec. 2, p. 1.

"Tragedy and the Common Man," *New York Times* (February 27, 1949), Sec. 2, pp. 1 and 3. Also printed in *Theatre Arts*, 35:48–50 (March 1951).

"The 'Salesman' Has a Birthday," *New York Times* (February 5, 1950), Sec. 2, pp. 1 and 3.

"Monte Saint Angelo," *Harper's*, 202:39–47 (March 1951). (Story.)

"Many Writers: Few Plays," *New York Times* (August 10, 1952), Sec. 2, p. 1.

"University of Michigan," *Holiday*, 14:41, 68–71, 128–32, 136–37, 140–43 (December 1953).

"A Modest Proposal for Pacification of the Public Temper," *Nation*, 179:5–8 (July 3, 1954).

"The American Theater," *Holiday*, 17:90–98, 101–2, 104 (January 1955).

"A Boy Grew in Brooklyn," *Holiday*, 17:54–55, 117, 119–20, 122–24 (March 1955).

"Picking a Cast," *New York Times* (August 21, 1955), Sec. 2, p. 1.

"The Family in Modern Drama," *Atlantic*, 197:35–41 (April 1956).

"Concerning the Boom," in *International Theatre Annual*, No. 1, edited by Harold Hobson. London: John Calder, 1956. Pp. 85–88.

"The Misfits," *Esquire*, 48:158–66 (October 1957). (Story.)

"Brewed in 'The Crucible,'" *New York Times* (March 9, 1958), Sec. 2, p. 3.

"The Shadows of the Gods," *Harper's*, 217:35–43 (August 1958).

"Bridge to a Savage World," *Esquire*, 50:185–90 (October 1958).

"My Wife Marilyn," *Life*, 45:146–47 (December 22, 1958).

"I Don't Need You Any More," *Esquire*, 52:270–309 (December 1959). (Story.)

"Please Don't Kill Anything," in *The Noble Savage*, No. 1. Cleveland and New York: World, 1960. Pp. 126–31. Also printed in *Redbook*, 117:48–49 (October 1961). (Story.)

"The Playwright and the Atomic World," *Tulane Drama Review*, 5:3–20 (June 1961).

"The Prophecy," *Esquire*, 56:140–41, 268–87 (December 1961). (Story.)

"Glimpse of a Jockey," in *The Noble Savage*, No. 5. Cleveland and New York: World, 1962. Pp. 138–40. (Story.)

"With Respect for Her Agony — But with Love," *Life*, 56:66 (February 7, 1964).

CURRENT AMERICAN REPRINTS

After the Fall. New York: Bantam. $.95.

All My Sons, in *Famous American Plays of the 1940s*, edited by Henry Hewes. New York: Dell. $.75.

The Crucible. New York: Bantam. $.95. New York: Compass (Viking). $1.25.
Death of a Salesman. New York: Compass. $1.25.
Focus. New York: Avon. $.60.
Incident at Vichy. New York: Bantam. $.95.
A View from the Bridge. New York: Bantam. $.95. New York: Compass. $1.25.

Bibliography

Eissenstat, Martha Turnquist. "Arthur Miller: A Bibliography," *Modern Drama,* 5:93–106 (May 1962).

Biographical and Critical Studies

In addition to the articles and books listed below the reviews of the New York drama critics might also be consulted. Although not always critically illuminating, they are invariably either interesting or amusing.

Allsop, Kenneth. "A Conversation with Arthur Miller," *Encounter,* 8:58–60 (July 1959).

Brandon, Henry. "The State of the Theatre: A Conversation with Arthur Miller," *Harper's,* 221:63–69 (November 1960). Also printed in Brandon's *As We Are.* New York: Doubleday, 1961.

Gassner, John. *The Theatre in Our Times.* New York: Crown, 1954. Pp. 342–48, 364–73.

Goode, James. *The Story of the Misfits.* Indianapolis: Bobbs-Merrill, 1963.

Hascom, Leslie. " 'After the Fall': Arthur Miller's Return," *Newsweek,* 63:49–52 (February 3, 1964).

Huftel, Sheila. *Arthur Miller: The Burning Glass.* New York: Citadel [1965].

McCarthy, Mary. "Naming Names: The Arthur Miller Case," *Encounter,* 8:23–25 (May 1957).

Popkin, Henry. "Arthur Miller: The Strange Encounter," *Sewanee Review,* 68:34–60 (Winter 1960).

Seager, Allan. "The Creative Agony of Arthur Miller," *Esquire,* 52:123–26 (October 1959).

Tynan, Kenneth. "American Blues: The Plays of Arthur Miller and Tennessee Williams," *Encounter,* 2:13–19 (May 1954). Also printed in Tynan's *Curtains.* New York: Atheneum, 1961. Pp. 257–66.

Welland, Dennis. *Arthur Miller.* New York: Grove, 1961.

Williams, Raymond. "The Realism of Arthur Miller," *Critical Quarterly,* 1:140–49 (Summer 1959).